BEFORE WINTER

Ray Givans

First printed and published in 2000
Grendon House
8 Laxay. Isle of Lewis. HS2 9PJ U.K.

Copyrights © Ray Givans 2000
All rights reserved

ISBN 1 898891 14 1
British Library Cataloguing in Publicaton Data.
A catalogue record for this book is available from the
British Library

For
Eileen, Andrew and Christopher

Acknowledgements:

To the editors of the following publications, where some of these poems appeared for the first time: *Acumen, Artyfact, Christianity & the Arts(U.S.), Cold Mountain Review(U.S.), Exile, New Hope International, Northwords, On Being Alive (Australia), Other Poetry, Seam, Studio (Australia), Third Way.*
The anthologies: *Christian Poetry, 1994; Freda Downie Memorial Anthology (St. Albans).*
Some of these poems were also awarded the following prizes: *The Jack Clemo Memorial Poetry Competition, 1995 (1st); Christianity & the Arts Poetry Competition, 1998.(2nd); Studio Open Poetry Competition, 1998. (2nd).*

CONTENTS

TITLE	PAGE
Harsh Land	1
The Sower, County Tyrone	2
Work Ethic	3
Bridget's Birthday	4
Rest In Peace	5
When Two Lives Meet	6
Drowning	7
Journalist's Conversation	8
Escape	10
Hole In A Bible	11
Parent And Child	12
Poet's Lament For A Dead Wife	13
Hi, It's Sunday Morning	14
Dead Child Contemplates Father	16
Cornfield With Cypress	17
A Day At The Races	18
Before Winter	20
Cherry Blossom	22

HARSH LAND.

In bed the warmth of early sun glances
over their wrinkled pillow, flowers across
their faces. Her cheeks are bruised; portwine
stains of age, and fault-lines cut beneath
the chin, serrate her loose-skin necklace.
Her arms are gloved around his shoulders, distended
fingers twisted. Daily, all her working
life she's hooked and chivvied pigs; excitable,
squealing, could turn with wet-snout snarl,
maul and fracture. These ill-set fingers,
fluid, serene, spider down his back.

His head, freckled like a thrush's breast
leans against her cheek. His beard's exuberance,
like a prophet in from wilderness, hides
the lips that held hard-won nails,
shaped a farmstead against a thrawn wind,
licking drumlin, cool moorland, heathers,
mosses, down to thin, stony soil: Galbally.
Here he struggled; seed-forgiving land
submitting harvest.
      His toughened fingers,
tendering her vertabrae, once wrote two hundred
love letters. She's stored them in this sanctuary.

They rise, wash off the night that closed
on their embrace; one body separates, gathers
daytime faces, passes the bedroom threshold.
heir folded nightgowns hold faint trace
of earth, await return, to ease around their
bodies; familiar, warm, protective skin.

     ***

THE SOWER, COUNTY TYRONE.

He lifts his kap in thanks for mornin sun;
turns, pulls the rim in shuttered concentration.
His boots are caked with dung; his hans are coorse,
that wark a land, hard-earned as watter
sprung from wells. The peaty sods rear up
like eels, blue-black, their furrowed track.
Across the trimmlin' skein of open fields
the boulders gurgle up from deep within.

Left fut furrit, arm outstretched, the poised
lone dancer, casts saft seed on fertile watters.
He leves the seed to die in winter's grave;
prays for mizzered win and rain, resuscitating
sun, for harvest corn, for met and plenty.
Each year the faur smoching town comes narrder.

kap = cap; coorse = coarse; wark = work; trimmlin' = trembling;
fut = foot; furrit = forward; saft = moist; mizzered = measured;
met = food; faur = distant; smoching = choking smoke;
narrder = nearer.

***

WORK ETHIC

The painter swings his pot of pale lavender,
gawks across the fence at our stooped neighbour:
'That's what I like to see, a man workin'.
I feel the calloused hands of my father, grandfather;
the slow drip from their brows.
Sweat from centuries of hardened stalactite
collects and wrinkles in my silken palms.
The sun rims my frail arms
as I lug brimming armfuls of hay;
listen to the well-versed swish
of my grandfather's pitchfork,
balletic swings, light, rhythmic,
as he stacks the conical mounds,
binds the sheaves with tight twine,
that stand and yellow, like rows of belted scarecrows.

And every man is expected to lend a hand;
no noble peasants here, held in sentimental pose.
Honest toil, sweat of the brow, hard labour.
Time presses, like dark clouds edging apple-green sky.
This is the season, the cycle, the farm, home.

Is this why my labour's furtive?
The poetry book lies face down on the coffee table.
My squat pen won't sweat; works like a burden of bad conscience.

***

BRIDGET'S BIRTHDAY.

My face is cracked; blue-purple
veins trace my sagged skin.
Sister Patricia tilts the card
to the camera. Her lips are glossed.
She smiles. My teeth have gone astray.

In gold letters, *one hundred and two*
hovers in a rose garden. Bees hum
around the white hawthorn. Bright
tortoise-shells flit in and out
of frail branches. Memories come, go.

Beyond I look out across the sweep
of yellow cornfields. I am standing
on my kitchen's warm stone flags.
Small windows let little light pass
from distant drumlins. Flames crackle

from the turf fire. I stroke its heart;
transplant a glow of embers to the hearth.
Aroma of warm bread. Forgetting winters,
failed seed, I spread the harvest bleach-
white flour sheet against a ripe field.

There are smiles on the faces that tend me.
I read the inscription: 'Best Wishes Always.'
Hidden from the camera my hand clutches
a photograph of a man whose lips
I cannot warm; his smile, too long frozen.

***

REST IN PEACE.

We met, only once, down a frost-blighted
tributary of 'Caulfield. The fire rasped, spat
splinters of turf, stacked against a chill night,
as a fidget stabbed out steel, where Mary sat.

The body lies waste, rimmed with lace, mummified.
The pastor, moss-stain bleaching his boots
speaks of Thomas with open bible or humbly
telling stories of his Monaghan roots.

And I smell this sweet-ringed halo of smoke
that falls on you, alone, tending neat borders;
hear a son speak of death's release, a broken
door, Alzheimer yells, gagged by orderlies.

***

WHEN TWO LIVES MEET.

Opposite, the woman scrubs as she kneels;
and from his wheelchair she seems pathetic
as her ungainly body grinds on wheels
driven by inbred Protestant ethic.

She fills days with lists of chores completed.
Never sleeps; yet, at night, dreams by the fire;
only her emotions are depleted,
surrogate mother, work feeds her desire.
And in her living is content.

Stooped, at work, she watches a life cheated
and has pity for inert arms and legs.
She thinks how his life must be depleted
for without work, he sits dog-bowed and begs.

And yet his mind wanders through wilderness,
sure-footed where great men sought enlightenment.
Even in his dreams he is whole no less
than when he walked upright, with thoughts head bent;
And in his being is content.

***

DROWNING

The family door closed, they hauled
the grocer's boy before the camera.
That morning she left the doctor's surgery,
stepped from sunlight to shadow across

one hungry street, passed the time
of day, as usual; dropped two tins
into her carrier bag...
                      A farmer's
eyes unraised from cold loam

did not hear the warmed engine whirr,
see her pass mallard, whin,
midged air, enter Eskra
dark water, updraught cool

before the coldness gripped her son.
He turned to question the mother
who spooned his food for thirty years.

A heart of corn, says the grocer's boy,
Brother ambushed, gunned to the head;
husband, dropped, lately, sudden.

That morning some tightened straws loosened
on her broad shoulders.
                    If God looked on
did he recall the dark brooding hour
of His Gethsemane? Did his fingers
search those murky waters, reach
                                  out,
                                          touch her?
        ***

JOURNALIST'S CONVERSATION

I tramped in cow dung; was greeted by a donkey's
breath streaming through a gap in a stable
door. A roll-sleeved midwife squeezed
a wet cloth, bathed the baby on her lap.

Squinting through brazing sun I saw
a figure recline against a red pallet. Two
tapped. The midwife came; claimed this *Mary*
was *virago intacta* – too exhausted for interview.

The husband was hunched under a fruitless fig
tree; dark, in shadow, eyes strained
on infertile soil. Unshaved, his clothes were stained
with sweat. And when I wafted the fat wad

of dollars he couldn't raise himself to take
them. (Now that's what I called 'suffering')
In the old days I'd delight as he squirmed
Like a fly swiped, delirious; the slow

pressure, the kill, the blood smear.....talked
of angels. I played my face like a straight bat.
Back at the office they kept a space for me
between the babe with sixty-six inch (enhanced)

chest and Earl from Connacht fronting flat-
earthers....yet, uneasy, queasy from slopping
out swill, weekly, to guzzlers of
the bizzare, of fiction, of lies, lies. So

I sneaked back, one night, before the Wise
Men rumbled the star; held the child.
Some seed stirred within my dead spirit
by an unseen aura, flamed by the child,

the suffering, enduring father. I took the risk,
resigned. My wife would rant, walk; and I
would walk a rugged path, waverer, back-
slider, disciple, seeking out that Promised Land
　　　　........................
Old, whiskered, once cynic, at Cana
I have tasted the good, good wine.

***

ESCAPE

(The poet, Khamphan Pradith, was interned in a labour camp, in Laos, 1979. Later, he managed to escape to Germany and was given refuge in the U.S.)

My pleasure is savouring of stamps,
tang of distant names, hard labour camps;
the tear of tape. Aid, wrapped and folded.

Our health is poor, the winters colder.

We taste cruelty: a dentist's vice
rings our neck; speared with bristling needless
our face deforms to twisted gargoyle.

I relish stars that break in Mekong's reeds,
the lorry, spilling juices, chicken soiled.

Our visa arrives. We fly and sit
huddled against a windy city;
I write me, the seal rimmed with spice.

***

HOLE IN A BIBLE

(Art exhibit, Dublin)

Hushed, in a shoulder-bag
  we cross O'Connell Street.
    Hustled crowds miss my muzzled protests.

In a converted warehouse
  hands warm my leather;
    finger-sweat white on my black spine.

Mute on the stone cold floor
  blue eyes interrogate.
    I doze. Dazed by the screech

drill, the bit bites
  into my tissue; the hole
    in my body Thomas-testing wide.

In front of a camera
  she is kindly, affable, smiles.
    This is my personal icon.

Outside, on the oil-black pavement
  the crowd, unconcerned, scurry home.
    Salman Rushdie slinks around a corner.

***

PARENT AND CHILD

You release my hand, lever yourself
down through ferns and bracken
to a moss and lichen floored glade,
shallow, winter sunlit stream,
cold stepping stones.
                      Stepping out
I call your name, *Christopher*...
remember how at your age, at the bottom
of our garden, I swashbuckled
through Brobdingnagian grasses, ill-
tempered nettles, to Blackwater.
In spate or shallow, its steeping stones
enticed, challenged. Free reined
I kept my eye looking forward
to where bowed cows nuzzled wet dock leaves.
Until, one day, nonchalant or playful
I'd lose my foothold; look back...
I ease the chain. You reach the bank,
trample sage, hurdle a gate, look back,
smile, disappear. One, two
minutes before I hear you hoot,
flood back. In harness, enfolded.

***

POET'S LAMENT FOR A DEAD WIFE

Before we parted the bread you took
from the oven sang. A rosary of candles

light the dark; Amergin[1] sings:
I am a thorn, grief beneath your flesh.

I tasted the Atlantic, salt wind
bitter at my back , as your cold

blue eyes wash my wine-stained
mouth, face of ill-cut stubble.

Your soul returns to encircle me
like a Celtic knot;
the ring that binds us is unbroken.

[1] BARDIC POET

***

HI, IT'S SUNDAY MORNING.

...this is brilliant...move on...over to you,   Zo:

In this photo of Nigel – sorry to show
this one Nige – you are caught with no collar on.
It was taken just after your ordination...
In a while we want all our viewers to phone
in about adultery, as you see it today.

I am looking forward to hearing your views,
but before that let's talk to our guest for today;
a warm welcome Meserra. Your musical roots
are in Afro-Caribbean gospel and mixed
with a spoonful of soul and a peppering of funk.
And, I believe, some of the lyrics touch on God:
So let's hear, 'And I cry when you take me so high.'

Had a caller from Croydon who says, 'In this day
and age it's expecting too much to remain
in a faithful, loving and stable relationship;
a large number of callers are saying the same.
I must say I liked Meserra's blue braids.

You are looking relaxed, reclining on that couch,
just at ease like a Sunday morning, there, Rog.
A number of viewers enjoyed your last poem.
Would be cool to make use of that cathedral
and get fans in a joyous mood for the Cup:
'Abide With Us'…..'God Save Our Gracious Team.'

On our next programme we want calls about coveting.
Do you envy your neighbour's ox or his/her Porsche?
Why not get on that phone and give us your views.

Many thanks there Tone, and for dangling the toes
in a paradise pool in Eilat. Well, can you
Adam and Eve it, the garden is just an allegory…
for the price of a pint we'll send a bible fun-pack.

Thanks too, Nige, Zo. So tune in again – find out more
about God, the universe and …ah…everything.

***

DEAD CHILD CONTEMPLATES FATHER

You watched me forceps hauled into the world,
first breath warm on damp uncurled fingers.
Now, you lay my clothes to rest upon the floor;
spread my pleated skirt and sweat-shirt,
form my body. Seed the open colouring book
with unused coins, framed by an angel's flame-

yellow aura. You squat in lotus, fingers
pack beneath your chin, assist prayer.
Shallow breath. Behind closed eyes, momentarily,
the dress flutters, fills with my cold flesh.
A shift in concentration punctuates the cloth.
A breath away, I cannot staunch the pain.

***

CORNFIELD WITH CYPRESS.

The cypress tree, fluid greens,
laps the orange-lemon corn,
jabs the dark compacted clouds.
A thin green middle-sea is go-
between for oil-rich sky, light
wash of land. Pale, distant
drumlins feel the wind-cool strokes
across their breasts. They mask
an evening lark; its song flight
cannot breach oppressive clouds.
The wind whimpers; waves plash

across the estuary of ripe corn.
Some days, I have stood waist-deep
in theses fields, faced the oblique-
wind synapse, that ignites in
flickering orange surface flames.
The clouds descend. On cold loam
kernels settle round my feet.
I look to hills, more distant,
for threads of light to penetrate the cracks.
And always, for hope, resuscitated seed;
the promise: all will be well, all will be well.

***

A DAY AT THE RACES

I settled the arrangement: the dark glazed
vase in the shape of a soup tureen;
laced it with carnations. The full blooms
flare like tu-tus (scents augmenting

my *Dior*), balanced on a cloth of Irish
linen; the crease running beneath
the *waterford* bowl, poised citrus.
My pearls warm against cool *Givenchy*.

Susan turns her green eyes to camera.
She is sleek as the crystal table-glass
from which she sips *Dom Perignom*.
Sam plucked her out at the Hilton;

wanted her most from all those scented
secretaries. She knew I saw her cool
fingers massage his neck, while I busied.
She helped take care of the sex *thing*.

Heard rumours of liaisons on the *Chantel*,
and imagined how suave he'd look in *Sulka* linen;
how sweet juice could ooze from his hard shell
and servants who wouldn't tell. Adored him.

You see the divide between Sam and me
and look beyond the round windows, sound-
proofed from the crowd, fun-seekers,
but, mostly, small-time punters

with dreams of fortune. Last furlong.
They melt down to the finishing line,
a rainbow coloured blur, with crop
of gold promise of their number on that

ticket, one day, the good life. Beneath
the table my fingers cling to the winners'
combination. Doors will open before me
as obsequious men in off-the-peg

suits will lead me to the V.I.P.
enclosure. I will pat the panting mare.
Mist will rise from her sweating flanks;
a few seasons she has her uses.

***

BEFORE WINTER

Candles burn
   gentle yellow
flames around
   my grave.
Yet, you cannot
   hear my del-
icious laughter
   thirty-four
dying of cancer
   the jokes
grew blacker to
   the last
for I could
   not die
any differently
   could not
clutch at super-
   natural straws.
The only God
   I knew was
my makeup artist.
   His foundations
changed my life.
   Yet, I had
my commitments
   the stripes
across my back
   holding the
picket line
   just causes.

Let me feel
    the warmth
of my husband's
    resusitating
lips; our child
    at my cold
breast. When he
    is older, tell
him, tell
    him how it is
here, ever-
    lasting disquiet,
without light
    without rest
without God.

        ***

CHERRY BLOSSOM

The flowers are hand-painted Belleek, parian cups
spilling yellow-honeyed seeds of flaked manna.
I stand beneath the canopy's umbrella, brilliant
as white-washed cottages, that furrow distant
illuminated hills across the oils of Belfast lough.
The shawl, embroidered white and greens, holds me.
Once, I would have struggled to break free,
fallen from grace into a dandelion and burdock soup,
where stinging nettles confer with wild-eyed clover.
I lean against your signatures of muscle, dark-sinewed arms
swim within your sinuous strands of fire-white beard,
and like the orange-beaked songbirds that blossom
on your wings, I will sing, sing, sing.

***